Nelson English
Workbook 5

This book belongs to

_____

Wendy Wren and Sarah Lindsay

OXFORD
UNIVERSITY PRESS

Great Clarendon Street, Oxford, OX2 6DP, United Kingdom

Oxford University Press is a department of the University of Oxford.
It furthers the University's objective of excellence in research, scholarship,
and education by publishing worldwide. Oxford is a registered trade mark
of Oxford University Press in the UK and in certain other countries.

Text © Wendy Wren and Sarah Lindsay 2018
The moral rights of the author have been asserted.

First published 2018

All rights reserved. No part of this publication may be reproduced, stored in a retrieval system, or transmitted, in any form or by any means, without the prior permission in writing of Oxford University Press, or as expressly permitted by law, by licence or under terms agreed with the appropriate reprographics rights organization. Enquiries concerning reproduction outside the scope of the above should be sent to the Rights Department, Oxford University Press, at the address above.

You must not circulate this work in any other form and you must impose this same condition on any acquirer.

British Library Cataloguing in Publication Data

Data available

ISBN: 978-0-1984-1992-1

10 9

Paper used in the production of this book is a natural, recyclable product made from wood grown in sustainable forests. The manufacturing process conforms to the environmental regulations of the country of origin.

Printed in India by Multivista Global Pvt. Ltd

Acknowledgements
Series consultant: John Jackman

Cover and inside illustrations by Q2A Media Services Inc.

Page make-up by Aptara

The publisher and authors would like to thank the following for permission to use photographs and other copyright material:

p40, 62, 63, 66: Shutterstock.

Contents

Unit 1	The Hare and the Tortoise	4
Unit 2	Swifter, Higher, Stronger	8
Unit 3	Wind Poems	12
Unit 4	When the Wind Blows	16
Unit 5	Walking on the Moon	20
Unit 6	Centaurus 1	24
Unit 7	Looking at the Sky	28
Unit 8	Holiday Destination	32
Unit 9	The Flight of Icarus	36
Unit 10	Birds' Wings	40
Unit 11	Changing Times	44
Unit 12	Growing a City	48
Unit 13	Visit Dinosaur World	52
Unit 14	The Old Forest	56
Unit 15	Rainforests in Danger	60
Unit 16	Undersea World	64
Unit 17	Shipwrecked!	68
	Glossary	72

UNIT 1 The Hare and the Tortoise

Vocabulary

Prefixes that make antonyms

Remember, **antonyms** are opposites.

The **antonyms** of some words are made by adding a **prefix**.
helpful **un**helpful   obey **dis**obey
responsible **ir**responsible   formal **in**formal
Remember, when you add a **prefix** to a word, you just add it!
Don't worry if it makes a double letter.

A Use a **prefix** to make a word that matches each clue. The first one has been done to help you.

1 the opposite of happy   _____unhappy_____
2 the opposite of regular   _____
3 the opposite of trust   _____
4 the opposite of fortunate   _____

B Write as many words as you can that begin with the prefix **dis**.

Punctuation

Direct speech

Remember the different ways we punctuate **direct speech**.
   "Right then," said Hare. "I challenge you to a race."
   "Well," said Tortoise, "you have never beaten me."

A Add all missing **punctuation marks** to each sentence.

1 Are Hare and Tortoise having a race asked Badger How exciting
2 I think so said Rabbit and I know who will win
3 Owl is the referee said Badger He will ensure it is a fair race

4

Spelling

e or no e?

Remember, when a **suffix** is added to a word ending in **e**:
- drop the **e** if the suffix begins with a vowel or is a **y**.
- keep the **e** if the suffix begins with a consonant.

Always remember there **can** be exceptions to the rule!

A Add **ing** to each of these words. Then write in your own words what happens to words ending in **e** when the suffix **ing** is added.

1. drive _____
2. continue _____
3. strike _____
4. receive _____
5. trace _____
6. glide _____
7. choose _____
8. separate _____

_____

_____

B Complete these word sums.

1. hope + ful = _____
2. scribble + er = _____
3. close + ure = _____
4. issue + ed = _____
5. bride + al = _____
6. place + ment = _____
7. create + ion = _____
8. organise + ed = _____
9. spite + ful = _____
10. write + er = _____

C Now write six of your own word sums using words ending in **e** and different suffixes. Try them out on a friend. Mark their answers.

1. _____ + _____ = _____

2. _____ + _____ = _____

3. _____ + _____ = _____

4. _____ + _____ = _____

5. _____ + _____ = _____

6. _____ + _____ = _____

Grammar

Verb tenses

The tense of a verb tells us **when** something happens – in the **past**, the **present** or the **future**.

Tense	Example
• present simple	I **challenge** you to a race.
• present progressive	He **is winning**!
• past simple	Hare **looked** at Tortoise in surprise.
• past progressive	Hare **was limbering** up.
• present perfect	I **have beaten** every animal.
• past perfect	Rabbit **had tried** but could not beat him.
• future	He **will win**.

A Write the tense of the **verb** in each sentence.

1 Hare is racing Tortoise. _____

2 Owl had started the race. _____

3 Tortoise accepted the challenge. _____

4 Hare has beaten Badger. _____

B Complete the table with **past tense verbs**.

Past simple	Past progressive	Present perfect	Past perfect
I walked	You _____	He _____	They _____
We ran	He _____	I _____	She _____
You tried	We _____	It _____	You _____
They watched	You _____	We _____	I _____

C Use these **past perfect tense verbs** in sentences of your own.

1 had reached _____

_____

2 had stopped _____

_____

Writing

Describing characters

The Hare and the Tortoise is a story about a boastful Hare and a modest Tortoise. Hare challenges Tortoise to a race. He is so sure he will win that during the race he takes a rest. Tortoise carries on walking and wins the race.

1 You are going to write a description of one of the other characters from the story *The Hare and the Tortoise*.

Owl   Badger   Rabbit

   a Which character are you going to describe? Tick one.

    Owl ☐   Badger ☐   Rabbit ☐

   b Write words and phrases that describe what your character **looks like**.

   c Write words and phrases to describe what your character's **personality** is like. You should use your imagination. Here are some ideas to help you:

- Owl has been chosen by the other animals to make sure that no one cheats in a race. What sort of character do you think he is?
- Hare has beaten Rabbit in other races. Is Rabbit a good loser or a bad loser?
- Hare has beaten Badger in other races. Is Badger a good loser or a bad loser?

UNIT 2 Swifter, Higher, Stronger

Vocabulary

Alphabetical order

> It is easy to find a word in a dictionary because the words are arranged in **alphabetical order**.
> Remember, if the words begin with the same letter, you need to look at the second, third or fourth letters in each word.
> These words are listed in alphabetical order. The letter in bold shows the letter each word is ordered by.
>
> **s**chool   **se**conds   **si**te   **sp**ent   **sp**ort   **st**and   **st**art

A Put these words in alphabetical order.

1
- television _____
- temperature _____
- tennis _____
- team _____
- teenager _____

2
- knit _____
- knead _____
- kneel _____
- know _____
- knot _____

Punctuation

Commas in lists

> When we write **a list** in a sentence we use **commas**.
> We join the **last two things** in the list with the conjunctions **and**, **but** or **or**.
>
> He won gold medals for the 100 metres, the long jump, the 200 metres **and** the 4 x 100 metres relay race.

A Add the missing **commas** and **conjunctions**.

1. I can't decide whether to try running swimming _____ long jump.
2. Some people are good at playing cricket running very fast _____ playing football.
3. Eric Liddell was British Jessie Owens was American _____ Usain Bolt is Jamaican.
4. The Olympic Games have been held in Paris London Rio _____ Berlin.

Spelling

eous, **ious**, **cious** and **tious** word endings

> Remember these rules when adding **ous** to words.
> - If the root word ends in **e**, we usually drop the **e** before adding **ous**.
>   fam**e**   fam**ous**
> - If the root word ends in **ge**, we usually keep the **e**.
>   coura**ge**   courag**eous**
> - If there is an **i** sound (as in b**i**t), it is usually spelt with a letter **i**.
>   var**i**ous
> - When adding the **ious** suffix, if the root word ends in **ce** there is usually a **c** before the **ious**.
>   gra**ce**   gra**cious**
> - If there is a family word that ends in **tion** then there is usually a **t** before the **ious**.
>   ambi**tion**   ambi**tious**

A Complete these words, adding either **ious**, **cious** or **tious**.

1. spa_____
2. nutri_____
3. cau_____
4. prev_____
5. ser_____
6. conten_____
7. cur_____
8. vi_____
9. obv_____

B Write three of the words from **Activity A** in your own sentences.

1. _____
2. _____
3. _____

C Complete these tables with your own words.

If you are unsure of a word ending, check the words in a dictionary.

Words ending in:	
eous	ious

Words ending in:	
cious	tious

Grammar

Verbs with prefixes

> Letters added to the front of a word are called a **prefix**.
> **out** (prefix) + **run** (verb) = **to outrun** (to run faster than)
> **dis** (prefix) + **obey** (verb) = **to disobey** (to not obey)
> **mis** (prefix) + **behave** (verb) = **to misbehave** (to behave badly)
> **over** (prefix) + **cook** (verb) = **to overcook** (to cook too much)

A Underline the **verb with a prefix** in each sentence.

1 I think my friend misunderstood the rules.

2 We disagreed about who was the greatest runner.

3 He overestimated how well the team would do.

B Choose a **prefix** from the box that can be used with both verbs in each question. Write the **new verbs**.

dis   mis   over

1 a trust _____   b place _____

2 a fill   _____   b pay   _____

3 a appear _____   b like   _____

C Choose three of the **new verbs** you formed in **Activity B**. Use them in **sentences** of your own.

1 _____

_____

2 _____

_____

3 _____

_____

Biographical sketches

1 Use this plan to help you find and organise facts about an athlete of your choice.

    a Which athlete have you chosen? _____

    b Make notes.

Find out:	Notes
What country does the athlete come from?	
When were they born?	
What sport do they do?	
Which Olympic Games have they competed in?	
What medals have they won?	
Any other interesting information.	

2 Using this information, write a **biographical sketch** about your chosen athlete.

_____

_____

_____

_____

_____

UNIT 3 Wind Poems

Vocabulary

Using hyphens

> **Hyphens** (-) are sometimes used to make **compound words**. Most of these are adjectives.
>
> For example: **fast-moving**
>
> **Hyphens** are also sometimes used to **join a prefix to a root word**, especially if the prefix ends in a vowel and the root word begins with one.
>
> For example: **co-operate**

A Look carefully at these hyphenated words. Sort the words into the correct columns in the table.

> co-own   well-known   re-enter   non-stop
> time-saving   re-emerge   sport-mad   quick-thinking

Compound words	Prefixed words

Punctuation

Apostrophes of contraction

> Remember that **will not** has the irregular contraction **won't**.

> Remember, **apostrophes** (') are used in **contractions** in place of a letter or letters that have been left out.
>
> **He's** asked us to stay inside.   he's = he has
> The **storm's** very bad.   storm's = storm is

A Write the **underlined** words as contractions.

1 I <u>could not</u> use my umbrella.   _____

2 <u>It has</u> blown that tree down.   _____

3 We <u>will not</u> be able to go out.   _____

4 <u>They are</u> telling people to be careful.   _____

Spelling

ull and ul word endings

> It is important to notice the sound **ull** and **ul** words make.
> Most **ul** and **ully** words are linked to the suffixes **ful** and **fully**.
>   p**ull**   use**ful**   use**fully**

A Add **ull** or **ul** to the gaps to make a word. Use a dictionary to check you have spelt the words correctly.

1 f_____
2 thoughtf_____
3 joyf_____y
4 usef_____
5 caref_____
6 p_____
7 wonderf_____
8 f_____y
9 gracef_____y
10 g_____
11 plentif_____
12 d_____

> Remember, when the suffix **ful** is added to a word ending in **y**, the **y** needs to change to an **i** before the suffix is added.

B Complete the word sums.

1 beauty + ful = _____
2 mercy + ful = _____
3 help + fu = _____
4 fancy + ful = _____
5 care + ful = _____
6 wonder + ful = _____
7 plenty + ful = _____
8 shame + ful = _____

C Write each of these words in a sentence.

1 skillful _____

2 plentiful _____

3 truthful _____

4 thankful _____

Grammar

Noun and verb agreement

> When we use a **singular noun** or **singular pronoun**, we must use a **singular verb**.
>
> **The wind blows.**
>
> When we use a **plural noun** or **plural pronoun**, we must use a **plural verb**.
>
> **The windows rattle.**
>
> We use **is/was** with **singular nouns** and **singular pronouns**.
>
> We use **are/were** with **plural nouns** and **plural pronouns**.

A Underline the **noun** or **pronoun** and the **verb** in each sentence.

Write **S** for singular or **P** for plural.

Remember, a **pronoun** stands in place of a noun.

singular OR plural?

1 The wind blows loudly.   _____

2 It is very strong.   _____

3 The branches move.   _____

4 Leaves blow about.   _____

B Underline the correct **verb** to finish each sentence,

1 I like/likes the wind.

2 The windows rattle/rattles.

3 The wind whisper/whispers.

4 The wind rush/rushes around.

C Use each of these **nouns** in a sentence followed by **is** or **are**.

1 eyes

_____

_____

2 trees

_____

_____

3 road

_____

_____

Writing

Personification

> When writers give human/animal qualities to non-living things, it is called **personification**.
>
> The wind **is angry**.
>
> The wind **stamps his feet**.
>
> The wind **is a wolf** that **sniffs** at doors.

Here are some **verbs** we usually use with humans.

beam	chatter	race	whisper
dance	roar	smile	glide

1 Use **verbs** from the box or verbs of your own to finish each line of the poem below.

   Line 1: What noises could you **hear** a river making?

   I heard the river _____ and _____.

   Line 2: What could you **see** flames doing?

   I saw the flames _____ and _____.

   Line 3: What could you **feel** the sun doing?

   I felt the sun _____ and _____.

   Line 4: What noises could you **hear** the sea making?

   I heard the sea _____ and _____.

2 Can you add two new lines to the poem, using your own verbs?

   I saw the stars _____ and _____ .

   I heard the trees _____ and _____ .

UNIT 4 When the Wind Blows

Vocabulary

Over-used words: nice

> Remember, **nice** is a very over-used word and you can usually find a better word to use instead.

A Complete these sentences, filling each gap with a more interesting word than **nice**.

1. The gentle wind provided a _____ relief from the high temperatures.
2. Meena wore a _____ dress to her brother's wedding.
3. The farmer was grateful for the _____ weather.
4. The _____ fireworks made everyone feel excited.
5. The small island was a perfect place for a _____ holiday.

B Write a sentence of your own using the word **nice**. Then rewrite the sentence replacing the word **nice** with a better word.

_____

_____

Punctuation

Commas for extra information

> Sometimes we want to put **extra information** in a sentence. When the extra information can be taken away and the sentence still **makes sense**, we can use **commas**.
> Sir Francis Beaufort, a naval officer, collected information about the wind.

A Rewrite each sentence, adding the **extra information** in a suitable place.

> Remember to use **commas** before and after the **extra information**.

1. Sentence: The wind uprooted the old tree.
   Extra information: blowing at Force 10

   _____

   _____

2. Sentence: The Beaufort Scale is still used today.
   Extra information: giving information about the wind

   _____

   _____

Spelling

Silent letters

> **Silent letters** often have another particular letter next to them.
> **kn**ock   an **n** often follows a silent **k**
> **wr**ite   an **r** often follows a silent **w**
> cli**mb**   an **m** often comes before a silent **b**
> ca**st**le an **s** often comes before a silent **t**

A Copy these words. Circle the **silent letter** and underline the letter that often comes either before or after it.

1 knees   _____   2 listen   _____
3 lamb   _____   4 wrong   _____
5 fasten   _____   6 numbness _____
7 knead   _____   8 wrinkled _____

B Write each of these words correctly. They each have a missing silent letter.

1 rap   _____   2 crum   _____
3 det   _____   4 reckage   _____
5 nown   _____   6 plumer   _____
7 whisle _____   8 lisen   _____
9 not   _____   10 ristwatch _____
11 thum   _____   12 neel   _____

C Write as many silent letter words as you can into a sentence.

_____
_____

Grammar

Noun round-up

There are different types of **nouns**.
- A **common noun** begins with a **small letter**.
    s**ailor**
- A **proper noun** begins with a **capital letter**.
    Francis **Beaufort**
- A **collective noun** is the name of a **group of things**.
    a **fleet** of ships
- A **compound noun** is made up of two words.
    weather-vane
- An **abstract noun** is the name of a **quality**, a **feeling**, an **idea**, or **time**.
    kindness

Nouns are naming words. **Abstract nouns** are the names of things you **cannot** see and touch.

A Write each **noun** from the box under the correct heading.

The first one is done for you.

~~Atlantic~~	crew	haircut	information	Beaufort
beauty	flock	weather-vane	fleet	bedroom
Pacific	bunch	downpour	honesty	fear
Philippines	happiness	newspaper	Francis	pack

Proper noun	Collective noun	Compound noun	Abstract noun
Atlantic			

B Use two **abstract nouns** from **Activity A** in sentences of your own.

1 _____

_____

2 _____

_____

Reports

1 You are going to write a **factual report** on the weather.

  a Look at each picture below. They show the effects of the wind at different times on one day, the 17th May.

7 a.m.   11 a.m.   3 p.m.   7 p.m.

  b Look at the following information from the Beaufort Scale and decide the force of the wind in each picture.

Force	Type of wind	What you can see	Speed
0	calm	smoke rises straight up	below 1 kph
4	moderate breeze	dust and paper blown around small branches move	20–29 kph
6	strong breeze	large branches move umbrellas are difficult to use	40–49 kph
10	storm	trees are uprooted	89–102 kph

  c Using the information from the pictures and the chart, make **notes** about the wind on 17th May.

date: _____   date: _____
time: _____   time: _____
strength of the wind: _____ strength of the wind: _____
speed of the wind: _____ speed of the wind: _____
effects of the wind: _____ effects of the wind: _____
_____ _____

date: _____   date: _____
time: _____   time: _____
strength of the wind: _____ strength of the wind: _____
speed of the wind: _____ speed of the wind: _____
effects of the wind: _____ effects of the wind: _____
_____ _____

2 Use your notes to help you write your report in your exercise book. The report should contain four paragraphs, one for each picture.

UNIT 5 Walking on the Moon

Vocabulary

Synonyms

> Remember, **synonyms** are words or phrases that have similar meanings. However, there are usually slight differences in meaning between synonyms. We can often rank a set of synonyms in order, from 'least' to 'most' based on the 'strength' of the word meaning.

A With a line, join all the synonyms that relate to the words on the left.

1. fly   quiet, remote, distant, isolated, solitary
2. lonely   aid, save, support, assist, rescue
3. help   soar, flutter, glide, shoot, zoom

B Look at these pairs of synonyms. Which would you rank 'least' out of:

1. quiet ☐   isolated ☐
2. assist ☐   rescue ☐
3. flutter ☐   soar ☐

Punctuation

Dashes for extra information

> Sometimes we want to put **extra information** in a **sentence**.
> When the extra information can be taken away and the sentence still **makes sense**, we can use **dashes**.
>   In 1969, three astronauts – Neil Armstrong, Buzz Aldrin and Michael Collins – were launched into space on the *Apollo 11* spacecraft.

A Rewrite each sentence, adding the **extra information** in a suitable place.

1. Sentence: The first human walked on the Moon in 1969.
   Extra information: Neil Armstrong

   _____

   _____

2. Sentence: Many people heard Aldrin's voice.
   Extra information: 600 million

   _____

   _____

Spelling

cial and **tial** word endings

> Words with **cial** and **tial** can be tricky to spell.
> Two rules worth remembering are:
> - **cial** usually comes after a vowel letter
> - **tial** usually comes after a consonant letter

A Add the correct **cial** or **tial** ending to each of these words.

1. spe_____
2. benefi_____
3. poten_____
4. cru_____
5. essen_____
6. offi_____
7. residen_____
8. confiden_____
9. superfi_____

B These words are exceptions to the rules. Write each of these words into your own sentences.

Remember to look up any words you don't know the meanings of in a dictionary.

1. initial _____
   _____

2. financial _____
   _____

3. commercial _____
   _____

C Find and copy the six **cial** and **tial** words in the word search.

x	t	c	r	u	c	i	a	l	f
a	z	r	f	c	o	v	j	d	e
r	p	e	h	b	n	d	p	r	s
t	m	y	q	l	f	h	d	n	s
i	p	a	r	t	i	a	l	k	e
f	x	n	w	r	d	t	y	v	n
i	t	p	t	j	e	m	z	b	t
c	j	i	n	i	t	i	a	l	i
i	y	s	s	f	i	n	x	p	a
a	n	y	f	q	a	b	p	e	l
l	j	t	o	w	l	a	n	r	y

_____

_____

_____

_____

_____

_____

Grammar

Modal verbs

> This group of **helper verbs** is very useful. These are called **modal verbs**.
>
> may   might   could   can   must   would   should
>
> He **can** fly   (is able to)   He **may** fly.   (has permission to)
> He **might** fly.   (it is possible)   He **must** fly.   (has to)
> He **could** fly.   (is able to)   He **would** fly.   (if it is possible)
> He **should** fly.   (ought to)

A Complete each sentence with **might** or **must**.

1 He _____ have to fly manually if the computer breaks down.

2 He _____ put on his moonsuit before he leaves the spacecraft.

3 The astronaut _____ wait in the space shuttle for the others to come back.

B Complete each sentence with **could**, **should** or **would**.

1 I _____ finish my homework before I go out.

2 I _____ finish my homework quickly if I just got on with it!

3 I _____ finish my homework if I could find the book I need.

C Use these **modal verbs** in sentences of your own.

1 can find _____

2 might arrive _____

3 should write _____

First person reports

When you write a **report** about something that has **happened to you**, you should:

- write in the **first person**
- use the **first paragraph** to say what you are going to write about
- present the **events in the order** in which they happened
- use a **formal style**
- use words and phrases to show the **passing of time**.

1 Imagine you are an astronaut who has walked on the Moon. You are going to write a **report** about the things that happened.

    a Your first paragraph
Include your name, who you were with, the date, the name of your spacecraft and what you were doing.

_____
_____
_____

    b Your second paragraph
Include the journey to the Moon's surface in the spacecraft, where you landed and the time.

_____
_____
_____

    c Your third paragraph
Include when you left the spacecraft, what you were wearing and what you did.

_____
_____
_____

    d Your fourth paragraph
Explain what you did when you were on the Moon's surface.

_____
_____
_____

    e Your fifth paragraph
Explain how you got back into the spacecraft.

_____
_____
_____

UNIT 6 Centaurus 1

Vocabulary

Synonyms for said

Remember, **synonyms** are words or phrases that have similar meanings.

When we write direct speech, it can be very boring to use **said** all of the time. There are lots of other words you could use.

A Choose the best **synonym** from the box to replace **said** in each sentence.

> explained   yelled   enquired   whispered

1 "You must be quiet," she said.   _____

2 "Look out!" he said.   _____

3 "This is how you do it," the teacher said.   _____

4 "Where are you going?" she said.   _____

B Write four more words you could use to replace the word **said**.

_____   _____   _____   _____

Punctuation

Commas to avoid ambiguity

Ambiguity is when a sentence could mean two very different things.

Using **commas** wrongly, or missing them out altogether, can make it very difficult for a reader to know exactly what you mean.

A Explain the different **meaning** of each pair of sentences.

1 a Slow, spaceships are approaching.

_____

   b Slow spaceships are approaching.

_____

2 a Hari likes space, travel and football.

_____

   b Hari likes space travel and football.

_____

24

Spelling

able, ible, ably, ibly word endings

> Remember, when the suffixes **able** (or **ably**) and **ible** (or **ibly**) are added to a root word ending in a single **e**, the **e** is usually dropped.
>
> val**e** + **able** = valuable
>
> Another clue to help you decide when to use **able** or **ible** is if the **antonym** of the word has a **prefix**.
> Usually if the prefix is **un**, it is an **able** word.
>
> **unbelievable**
>
> Usually if the prefix is **in**, **il** or **ir**, it is an **ible** word. For example:
>
> **invisible**

A Write the correct **able** or **ible** ending to complete the words.

1. prob_____
2. unrecognis_____
3. lov_____
4. unwork_____
5. valu_____
6. us_____
7. incred_____
8. horr_____
9. depend_____
10. ed_____
11. miser_____
12. irrespons_____

B Write two more **able** words.

_____   _____

Write two more **ible** words.

_____   _____

C Now use two of the words you made in **Activity B** in sentences of your own.

a _____

_____

b _____

_____

Grammar

Interesting adjectives

> We always need to read through what we write to see if we can **improve** it. It is easy to use boring **adjectives**.
>
>   It was **nice** on board the spaceship.
>
> Using a **synonym** instead of a boring adjective makes our writing more interesting.
>
>   It was **familiar/secure/comfortable/safe** on board the spaceship.

A Underline the **interesting adjective** in each sentence.

1 The huge spaceship left Earth.
2 The angry crew wanted to turn back.
3 They listened to the ancient message.

B Copy and complete each sentence with a more **interesting adjective** than the **adjective in bold**.

1 The planet looked **small**.

_____

2 It could be a **bad** place.

_____

3 It might be **cold**.

_____

4 It might be **hot**.

_____

5 It might be **nice**.

_____

C Use these **interesting adjectives** in sentences of your own.

> Use a dictionary to help you.

1 strange _____

_____

2 wonderful _____

_____

Play scripts

1. You are going to write **the next scene** of the play *Centaurus 1*. The play is set aboard a spaceship that is on its way to a distant planet.

   The previous scene ended like this:

   [*The captain places the CD in the machine. The crew leans forward to listen.*]

   Voice from CD: To the crew of *Centaurus 1*, I have an important message …

   a Write **brief notes** on what you think the message could be about.

   _____

   _____

   _____

   b Read the information in this table, which shows how each member of the crew reacts to the message.

Character	What he/she thinks
Captain Fermi	insists they continue on their mission doesn't give reasons expects to be obeyed
Grant	angry doesn't think what they have heard makes any difference wants to turn back
Peter Bibikov	calm and reasonable tries to see the advantages and disadvantages of going on or turning back
Don	frightened doesn't want to go beyond the point of no return
Michelle	doesn't think there is anyone left on Earth to go back to
Margaret	uncertain and confused wants to take a vote on what to do

   c Use the information in the table to write the **next scene** in your exercise book. Remember to:

   - decide where the characters are, and write a short **scene** description.
   - set out your play script with the **characters names** on the left and the **dialogue** on the right.
   - use **stage directions** to show the actors:
     - how to behave
     - how to say their lines.

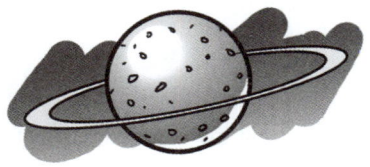

UNIT 7 Looking at the Sky

Vocabulary

Figures of speech

> An **idiom** is a short phrase that usually means something quite different from what you might expect.
> A **simile** is when something is described **as** or **like** something else.
> A **metaphor** is when something is described as if it **is** something else.

A Use a word from the word box to complete each of these **idioms**.

> cover   blue   boat   shoulders

1. an old head on young _____
2. can't judge a book by its _____
3. missed the _____
4. out of the _____

B Write a simile. _____

C Write a metaphor. _____

Punctuation

Possessive nouns

> **Possessive nouns** tell you who **owns** something.
> Singular possessive nouns   the **Sun's** centre
> Plural possessive nouns that end in s   the **stars'** light
> Plural possessive nouns that do not end in s   the **people's** glasses

A Underline the **owner** in each phrase.
Write **S** if the owner is singular or **P** if the owner is plural.

1. our solar system's galaxy _____   2. the stars' energy _____
3. the Sun's light _____   4. the planets' moons _____

B Write a sentence of your own using a **plural possessive noun**.

_____

Spelling

ir and ire words

> It is important to notice the distinctive sounds **ir** and **ire** words make.
>
> The Sun is like a huge ball of **fire**.
>
> A solar eclipse is an amazing sight but the **first** thing to remember is not to look straight at it.

A Use each of these **ir** words in your own sentences.

1 circle _____
2 birthday _____
3 dirt _____
4 thirsty _____

B List three more **ir** words.

_____   _____   _____

C Find seven **ire** words in the word search and write a definition for each one.

You can use a dictionary to help you.

h	t	i	r	e	d	g	y
t	t	m	e	r	e	e	a
a	q	r	t	w	g	x	c
b	w	f	i	r	e	p	q
e	t	p	r	e	y	i	u
g	k	g	e	s	t	r	i
i	n	s	p	i	r	e	r
p	e	r	s	p	i	r	e

_____   _____
_____   _____
_____   _____
_____   _____
_____   _____

Grammar

Forming verbs from nouns and adjectives

Some **verbs** are formed from nouns and adjectives by adding **suffixes**.
 ate   en   ify   ise

Noun	Verb
education	educate
strength	strengthen
beauty	beautify
energy	energise

Adjective	Verb
sharp	sharpen
simple	simplify
equal	equalise
pure	purify

A Underline the **verb** in each sentence.

Remember, some **verbs** are more than one word.

1 I was captivated by the solar eclipse.

2 The sky lightens at sunrise.

3 I am energised when the sun shines!

4 Can you simplify the information for me?

B Do the word sums to make **verbs**. Use each **verb** in a sentence of your own.

Check the spelling of the **verb** in a dictionary.

1 solid + ify = _____
Sentence: _____
_____

2 television + ise = _____
Sentence: _____
_____

3 strength + en = _____
Sentence: _____
_____

C Use these **verbs** in sentences of your own.

Use a dictionary to help you understand their meaning.

1 simplify _____
_____

2 widen _____
_____

Writing

Explanations

1 **a** Look carefully at the **diagram**.

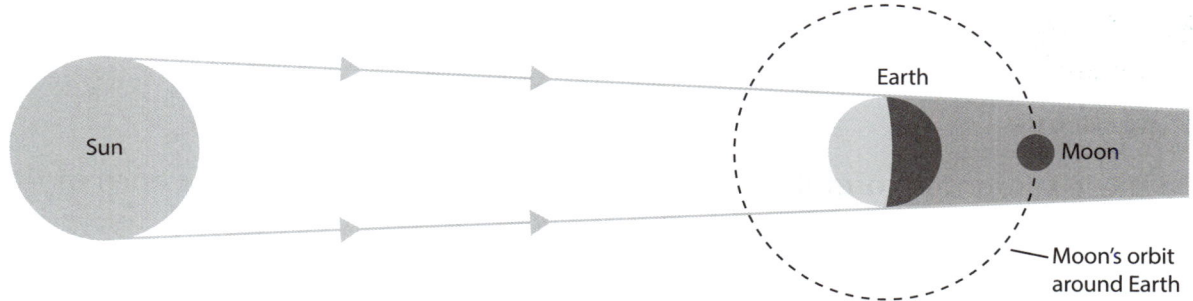

b Choose the correct words from the box to complete the short explanation below. You will need to use some words more that once.

| Moon   straight   Sun   Earth   shadow |

In a lunar eclipse, the _____, the _____ and the _____ are all in a _____ line. The _____ is between the _____ and the _____. The _____ is in _____ of the _____.

2 Choose **one** of the following:

- how a seed grows into a flower

- how rain clouds are formed

Plan an **explanation** by adding notes and a diagram.

_____

_____

_____

_____

_____

_____

UNIT 8 Holiday Destination

Vocabulary

Using a thesaurus

A Read these sentences carefully. Use a thesaurus to find a synonym for each of the words in bold.

1 Sri Lanka is a **beautiful** island in the Indian Ocean. _____

2 Its wildlife is **spectacular**. _____

3 The Bambarakanda Falls is the **highest** waterfall in Sri Lanka. _____

B Now use a thesaurus to find antonyms of the words in bold in **Activity A**.

1 _____   2 _____   3 _____

Punctuation

Indirect speech

> **Indirect speech** is when we write **about** what someone has said.
> We **don't** use the exact words.
> We **don't** use speech marks.
> Some visitors to the island say it is one of the most beautiful places on Earth.

A Change these sentences into **indirect speech**.

The first one is done for you.

1 "Have you been to Sri Lanka?" she asked.

   <u>She asked if I had been to Sri Lanka.</u>

2 "I went to Sri Lanka last year," I told her.

   _____

3 "Did you like the island?" she asked.

   _____

4 "I thought it was beautiful," he said.

   _____

5 "I agree," she said.

   _____

Spelling

fer words + suffixes

There are a few words that end in **fer**. For example:

refer   defer   transfer

When you add a suffix that begins with a vowel to a **fer** word, you need to **double** the r at the end of the word, if the **fer** is stressed.

re**fer** + **ing** = refe**rr**ing

re**fer** + **ence** = refe**r**ence

A Using the **suffixes** in the word box, add as many suffixes as you can to each of these root words.

Check in a dictionary that you have spelt each new word correctly and that you understand what each word means.

ence   ing   ed   al

1 refer

2 transfer

3 defer

B Write three of the new words you have made in **Activity A** in sentences of your own.

1 _____

2 _____

3 _____

33

Grammar

Relative pronouns

> **Relative pronouns** are special because they do two jobs.
> 1 They take the place of nouns.
> 2 They act like conjunctions, and they are related to the noun that comes before them in a sentence.
>
> Here are some common **relative pronouns**:
>   who   which   that
>
> **Who** is used for people.
>   There are many kilometres of golden sands. People just want to relax.
>   There are many kilometres of golden sands for people **who** just want to relax.
>
> **Which** and **that** are used for animals and things.
>   This is a travel brochure. It gives information about Sri Lanka.
>   This is a travel brochure **which/that** gives information about Sri Lanka.

A Underline the **relative pronoun** in each sentence.

1 I would like a holiday that is exciting.

2 That is the man who flies the seaplane.

3 I want to visit the beach that has the best surfing.

B Copy and join each pair of sentences with **who**, **which** or **that**.

1 This is my friend. He has visited Sri Lanka.

_____

2 We went on a train. It took us from Colombo to Jaffna.

_____

3 Here is a photo. We took it at sunset.

_____

C Write sentences about these things using **who**, **which** or **that**.

1 the seaplane _____

_____

2 visitors _____

_____

3 a dolphin _____

_____

Writing

Writing to inform and persuade

1. You are going to create a **brochure** about a place you would like to visit or have visited. Research **information** about the place.

    - What place have you chosen for you brochure? _____

    - Where is it? _____

    - What places of interest have you found for people to see. Choose three or four.

        _____   _____

        _____   _____

    - What words and phrases will you use instead of **nice**?

        _____ _____ _____   Use a thesaurus to help you.

        _____ _____ _____

    - What activities can people do when they visit? Make a list.

        _____   _____   _____

        _____   _____   _____

    - What words and phrases could you use to persuade people to do these things?

        _____   _____   _____

        _____   _____   _____

    - Are there any other details you would like to include, such as the food and the weather?

        _____

        _____

        _____

    - Brochures usually include photographs. What photographs do you want to include?

        _____

        _____

        _____

UNIT 9 The Flight of Icarus

Vocabulary

Homophones

Remember, **homophones** are words that sound the same, but are spelt differently and have a different meaning. For example:

Daedalus could **see** Icarus falling towards the **sea**.

A Write a definition for each of these **homophones**.

1 led _____
   lead _____
2 brake _____
   break _____
3 stationary _____
   _____
   stationery _____
   _____

Punctuation

Split direct speech

When we use **direct speech**, sometimes we **split the spoken words** so we have to be very careful about the **punctuation**.

two sentences: "Icarus, my son, come back!" **pleaded Daedalus.** "The sun will melt the wax!"

one sentence: "If you fly too low," **he said**, "the spray from the waves will make your wings wet and heavy."

A Add the **speech marks** and other missing **punctuation**.

1 You cannot go home said the King You must stay here and invent things for me
2 We have to escape said Daedalus I have to think of a plan
3 I have collected lots of feathers said Icarus and put them in your workshop
4 First I must make a wooden frame explained Daedalus and then melt the wax
5 Don't fly too low said his father Don't fly too high

Spelling

ow words

> The **ow** letter pattern can make different sounds.
> It is worth remembering that most words ending in **ow** have the **long o sound**, as in **go**.

A What am I? Use a word from the box.

| elbow | shadow | yellow | rainbow |
| narrow | pillow | window | burrow |

1. I'm a colour. _____
2. You can rest your head on this. _____
3. You see me when the sun shines. _____
4. I am the opposite to wide. _____
5. I'm home to a family of rabbits. _____
6. You can see through me. _____
7. I'm a part of your arm. _____
8. I'm multi-coloured and appear in the sky. _____

B Sort these words into the correct column of the table. Check each **syllable** has a vowel sound.

> Remember, a **syllable** is a part of a word that can be sounded by itself. Each syllable has its own vowel sound.

| grow | narrow | following | rainbow | window | shallow |
| tomorrow | arrow | own | mower | borrowing | hollow |

Words with one syllable	Words with two syllables	Words with three syllables

C Add one more **ow** word to each column of the table in **Activity B**.

Grammar

Sequencing adverbs

> **Adverbs** that tell us **the order in which things are done** are very useful for writing stories.
>
> Writing would be very repetitive if we only used **and then**.
>
> > Our teacher read us a story about Daedalus and Icarus **and then** we wrote a play about it **and then** we acted it out.
>
> There are more interesting words and phrases to show the sequence of events. These are called **sequence adverbs**.
>
> > **In the afternoon**, our teacher read us a story about Daedalus and Icarus. **Afterwards**, we had to write a play and act it out.

A Underline the **sequence adverbs** in these sentences.
1. Finally, Daedalus came up with a plan to escape from the tower.
2. Firstly, he sent Icarus to collect birds' feathers.
3. Meanwhile, he made a wooden frame in the shape of a bird's wing.
4. Afterwards, he melted some wax.
5. Next, Daedalus gave Icarus some advice.

B Rewrite this sentence replacing **and then** with more interesting words and phrases.

She went to the park **and then** she saw her friends **and then** they played on the swings **and then** they went home.

> You can make this into more than one sentence. You can put **sequence adverbs** at the beginning of sentences.

_____

_____

_____

_____

C Write three things you do before school each day, and put each one into a sentence. Use interesting words and phrases to show the order in which you do them.

1. _____

_____

2. _____

_____

3. _____

_____

Writing

Characters' thoughts and feelings

Daedalus and his son Icarus are being held captive by the King of Crete. Daedalus has made some wings so he and his son can escape from the island.

1 Imagine you are Icarus and it is the night before you are going to escape by flying out of the tower. Think about how you are **feeling**.

    a Are you feeling excited? Why?

    b Are you feeling frightened? Why?

    c Are you thinking about what life will be like when you escape? What will you do?

    d Are you thinking about what might go wrong? What could go wrong?

    e What are your last thoughts before you go to sleep?

UNIT 10 Birds' Wings

Vocabulary

Antonyms

> Remember, **antonyms** are words that mean the opposite. For example:
> fast   slow   maximum   minimum   broad   narrow
> Some words do not have an antonym.   bird   glide

A Write three words in each box.

Words with antonyms [ ]

Words without antonyms [ ]

B Choose two of the words with antonyms from **Activity A**. Write the words and their antonym into two sentences.

1 _____

2 _____

Punctuation

Brackets for extra information

> Sometimes we want to put **extra information** in a **sentence**. When the extra information can be taken away and the sentence still **makes sense**, we can use **brackets**.
> An albatross **(a type of seabird)** has very long wings.

A Rewrite each sentence, adding the **extra information** in a suitable place.

1 Sentence: This is the book I borrowed from the library.

   Extra information: a bird encyclopedia

   _____

   _____

2 Sentence: Sparrows can twist and turn quickly.

   Extra information: and other birds with short wings

   _____

Spelling

ough words

The letter pattern **ough** can be a tricky one to use as it makes a number of different sounds.

A Copy the **ough** words from the box that rhyme with the word at the top of each column.

bough   enough   brought   sought   cough   plough
rough   bought   though   trough   dough   thought

puff	off	toe	now	caught

B Each of these words has a **homophone** with the **ough** letter pattern. Write the **ough** word.

Remember, **homophones** are words that have the same sound but have a different meaning and spelling.

1 bow _____   2 sort _____

3 threw _____   4 doe _____

C Choose three **homophone pairs** from **Activity B**, and write a sentence using each pair.

You can use a dictionary to help you.

1 _____

_____

2 _____

_____

3 _____

_____

Grammar

Possessive pronouns and possessive adjectives

> **Possessive adjectives** describe **nouns**.
> This is **my** garden.
> These are **possessive adjectives**.
> my   your   his   her   its   our   their
> **Possessive pronouns** stand in place of a **possessive adjective + a noun**.
> This garden is **mine**. (mine = my garden)
> These are **possessive pronouns**.
> mine   yours   his   hers   ours   theirs

A Underline the **possessive pronoun** in each sentence.
1. This book about kingfishers is mine.
2. The jacket with birds on is hers.
3. Are those bird books ours?
4. This drawing is better than mine.

B Use a **possessive pronoun** instead of the underlined words in each sentence.

> The first one is done for you.

1. This tree <u>belongs to us</u>.
   <u>This tree is ours.</u>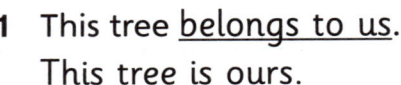

2. That camera <u>belongs to him</u>.
   _____

3. Those bird books <u>belong to them</u>.
   _____

4. Those photographs <u>belong to her</u>.
   _____

C Use each **pair of possessive adjectives** in a sentence of your own.
1. his   her
   _____

2. our   their
   _____

Bibliography

1. Choose an animal to research. Here are some suggestions.

   tiger   **bee**   **kangaroo**   **tortoise**

   a What animal have you chosen to write about? _____

   b Make notes on what you **already know**. _____

   _____
   _____
   _____
   _____

   c Do your **research** and make **notes** on new information. _____

   _____
   _____
   _____
   _____
   _____
   _____
   _____

2. Make a **bibliography**.

Author	Book title or name of website

UNIT 11 Changing Times

Vocabulary

Adverbs

 Many adverbs end in **ly**.

Remember, **adverbs** tell us more about verbs.
They usually tell us **how**, **when** or **where** actions happen.

A Complete each sentence by adding an **adverb** made from the word in brackets.

1 She read the map _____ (careful).

2 She found the bus stop _____ (easy).

3 The traffic moved _____ (slow).

4 The bus driver _____ (helpful) pointed the way.

5 She thought she would _____ (probable) visit the museum tomorrow.

B Write two of your own sentences using **adverbs** to give more information about the verbs.

1 _____

2 _____

Punctuation

Apostrophe round-up

An **apostrophe of contraction** shows where a letter or letters have been missed out.
  We're visiting the city.   (We are)
An **apostrophe of possession** shows that someone or something owns something.
  The **city's** streets are busy.   (the streets belonging to the city)

A Add the missing **apostrophes**.

1 theyre
2 the trains engine
3 the towns roads
4 shouldnt
5 the peoples houses
6 youve
7 the horses tails
8 Ive

Spelling

ant, **ent**, **ance**, **ence** word endings

Many adjectives end with **ent** or **ant**.
  differ**ent**   dist**ant**
These words can be made into abstract nouns by changing **ent** endings to **ence**, and **ant** endings to **ance**.
  differ**ence**   dist**ance**

A Complete the puzzle by filling in all the words from the word box. No word is used twice.

descent	ignorance	convenient	elegance	efficient
impatience	tolerant	impertinent	arrogant	tolerance
impatient	ignorant	impertinence	elegant	convenience

Grammar

Plural round-up

Singular nouns are made plural in different ways.

Noun	Singular/Plural
For most nouns, add an **s**	building/build**s**
For nouns ending in **s, ch, sh** and **x**, add **es**	bus/bus**es**
For nouns ending in **f** and **fe**, change the **f** or **fe** to **v** and add **es**	life/li**ves**
For nouns ending in **consonant + y**, take off the **y** and add **ies**	family/famil**ies**
For nouns ending in **vowel + y**, just add **s**	boy/boy**s**
For some nouns ending in **o**, add **es** For musical nouns ending in **o**, add **s** For nouns ending in **oo**, add **s**	potato/potato**es** cello/cello**s** kangaroo/kangaroo**s**
Some nouns are **different** in the plural form	foot/f**ee**t
Some nouns are **always** in the plural form	clothes

A Make each noun **plural**.

1 chimney _____   2 baby _____

3 brush _____   4 leaf _____

B Choose two plural nouns from **Activity A** to use in sentences of your own.

1 _____

2 _____

C Complete the label for each picture with a word that is always plural.

1

t_____

2

g_____

3

s_____

4

h_____

Writing

Using contrast

1. You are going to write a **poem** with **two verses**.
   The first verse should be about a park during the day.
   The second verse should be about the park at night.

   a Complete this word web, adding words you could use to describe the park during the day.

   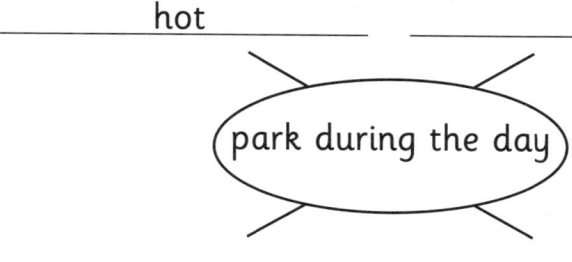

   _____ hot _____   _____

   (park during the day)

   _____   _____

   b Complete this word web, adding words you could use to describe the park during the night.

   _____ deserted _____   _____

   (park at night)

   _____   _____

   c Think of some words you could use to show that you **enjoy** being in a busy, crowded park during the day.

   excited   _____   _____   _____

   d Think of some words you could use to show that you do **not enjoy** being in a busy, crowded park during the day.

   noisy   _____   _____   _____

   e Think of some words you could use to show that you **enjoy** being in an empty park at night.

   calm   _____   _____   _____

   f Think of some words you could use to show that you do **not enjoy** being in an empty park at night.

   bored   _____   _____   _____

2. Use your words to write your poem in your exercise book.

UNIT 12 Growing a City

Vocabulary

Adverbs

> **Adverbs** tell us more about verbs. They usually tell us how, when or where actions happen.
> Remember, **adverbs** can tell us how words are spoken.
> They add detail and interest to your writing.
> "Let me help you," she said **kindly**.

A Write three **adverbs** that can be used with each of these verbs.

1 called _____ _____ _____

2 ran _____ _____ _____

3 wrote _____ _____ _____

B Use the verb and an adverb from **Activity A** in sentences of your own.

1 _____

2 _____

3 _____

Punctuation

Commas, dashes and brackets for extra information

> Sometimes we want to put **extra information** in a **sentence**.
> When the extra information can be taken away and the sentence still **makes sense**, we can use **commas**, **dashes** or **brackets**.
> The world's largest man-made harbour **(at Jebel Ali)** was created.

A Rewrite each sentence, adding the **extra information** in a suitable place.

1 Sentence: Dubai began with 800 members of the Bani Yas tribe.
 Extra information: in 1833

 _____

2 Sentence: By 1930, the city had grown enormously.
 Extra information: population 20,000

 _____

3 Sentence: The leader at the time ordered that the creek should be dredged.
 Extra information: Sheikh Rashid bin Saeed Al Maktoum

 _____

48

Spelling

ie and ei words

> Remember the rule:
>   **i** comes before **e** (when the sound is **ee**) except after **c** or when the sound is not **ee**
> For example:
>   rel**ie**ve   re**ce**ive   le**i**sure

A Write four **ie** and four **ei** words.

_____   _____

_____   _____

_____   _____

_____   _____

B Now make your own word search. Put the words from **Activity A** in your word search first, then add other letters to fill the gaps.

C Ask a friend to try your word search, remember to cover the words at the top of this page!

Grammar

Relative pronouns

> A **pronoun** takes the place of a **noun**.
>   The **creek** silted up.   **It** silted up.
> These pronouns are called **relative pronouns**.
>   who   which   that
> **Relative pronouns** are related to the noun that comes before them in a sentence.
>   Dubai is a city **that** developed very quickly.
> **who** is used for people   **which/that** are used for animals and things

A Underline the **relative pronoun** in each sentence.

1 I would like to visit a city that is near the desert.

2 This is the man who works in the market.

3 I would like to visit the hotel which is the tallest in the world.

B Copy and join each pair of sentences with **who**, **which** or **that**.

1 John is my friend. He has visited Dubai.

   _____

   _____

2 I went to Jebel Ali. It has a man-made harbour.

   _____

   _____

3 This is the book. It has interesting photographs of Dubai.

   _____

   _____

C Write sentences about these things using **who**, **which** or **that**.

1 a market _____

   _____

2 a sporting event _____

   _____

Flow diagram – key dates and events

1 Read the **summary** of the growth of Dubai, the capital of the United Arab Emirates.

> In 1833, 800 members of the Bani Yas tribe settled at the mouth of a creek on the coast of the Arabian Gulf. By the early 20th century, Dubai was a successful port with a large and busy market. By 1930 the population was 20,000.
>
> However, in the 1950s, the creek began silting up. Ships could not easily get into the harbour and trade was threatened. The leader at the time, Sheikh Rashid bin Saeed Al Maktoum, ordered that the creek should be dredged. This was a success, and made Dubai the major trading port in the area. Dubai continued to expand rapidly, and this was helped by the discovery of oil in 1966. By the 1980s and 1990s, Dubai's aim was to become a major tourist centre. In 2010, the Burj Khalifa, the tallest man-made structure on Earth, was completed.

2 Find the events that happened on these dates and complete the **flow chart** by writing brief notes in each box.

1833
800 members of the Bani Yas tribe settled at the mouth of a creek in the Arabian Gulf.

Early 20th century
Dubai was a successful port.

1930

1950s

1966

1980s and 1990s

2010

51

UNIT 13 Visit Dinosaur World

Vocabulary

Abbreviations and acronyms

> We often use shortened forms of words. There are called **abbreviations**.
>   phone = telephone
>
> Some groups of words can be shortened by using just the first letter or few letters of each of the main words. This is called an **acronym**.
>   **UN** is an acronym for **U**nited **N**ations.

A With a line, match each abbreviation with its word.

approximately	Dr
February	petrol
kilogram	adv
mathematics	kilo
petroleum	approx.
doctor	Feb
adverb	maths

The first one is done for you.

B Write three acronyms and the words they represent.

1 ____UN____ = United Nations _____
2 _____ = _____
3 _____ = _____

Punctuation

Commas between adjectives

> When we use two or more **adjectives** together, we may need to use a **comma**.
> Featuring the **biggest, scariest** dinosaur ride in the world!

Remember to add a **comma**.

A Add **two adjectives** to complete each sentence.

1 It was the _____ _____ ride I have ever been on!
2 The _____ _____ advertisement was interesting.
3 We won't go to the theme park on a _____ _____ day.
4 The _____ _____ child enjoyed the ride.

Spelling

ei and ie words

> Remember the rule:
>   **i** comes before **e** (when the sound is **ee**) except after **c** or when the sound is not **ee**
> For example:
>   rel**ie**ve   rec**ei**ve   l**ei**sure

A Add **ie** or **ei** to make a word.

1 v____n   2 h____ght   3 ____ghty   4 sh____ld
5 br____f   6 retr____ve   7 rec____pt   8 n____ther
9 bel____f   10 n____gh   11 shr____k   12 misch____f

B Circle the words in the box in which the **ie** or **ei** sounds like **ee**.
Underline those you have circled that have an **ei**.

their	shield	freight
field	deceit	believe
receive	rein	achieve
leisure	wield	chief
vein	eight	receipt

C Answer these questions.

1 What do you notice about the words you have underlined?
_____
_____

2 What do you notice about the words you haven't underlined or circled?
_____
_____

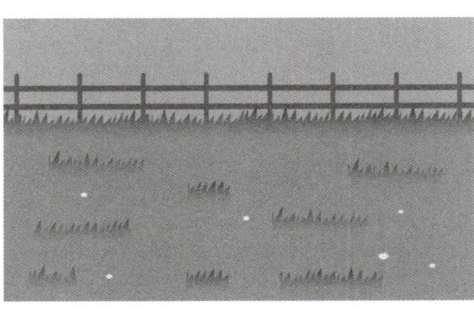

Grammar

Expanded noun phrases

> A **noun phrase** can include:
> - a definite article **the** Internet
> - indefinite article **a** ride/**an** advertisement
> - a demonstrative adjective:
>   singular **this** park **that** web page
>   plural **those** tickets **these** pictures
> - adjectives the **biggest, scariest** dinosaur
> - how many/how much **some** people/**a lot of** posters

A Underline the **noun phrases** in each sentence.

> There may be more than one **noun phrase** in a sentence. Look carefully!

1. This sunny day is perfect for a visit to the theme park.
2. The big, fierce dinosaur stared down at us.
3. Lots of unhappy people sheltered from the rain.

B Make each of these verb family names into an *ing* **adjective**. Then use the adjectives as part of a **noun phrase**. Add a **noun** to make a **noun phrase**.

> The first one is done for you.

verb family name	adjective	noun phrase
1 to excite	exciting	an exciting ride
2 to interest	_____	_____
3 to tire	_____	_____

C Add two words to each of these nouns to make **noun phrases**. Use each **noun phrase** in a sentence.

1. _____ highway

   Sentence: _____

2. _____ television

   Sentence: _____

3. _____ magazine

   Sentence: _____

4. _____ children

   Sentence: _____

54

Writing

Advertisements: a poster

1 You are going to design your own **poster**.

   a What is your poster **advertising**? Tick **one**.

   water park ☐   sports/hobby magazine ☐   healthy fruit drink ☐

   b Who is your advertisement aimed at? Tick **one**.

   Do you want children to see it and persuade their parents to take them/buy the product? ☐

   Do you want parents to see it and think it is an interesting place or product for their children? ☐

   c How will you make your advertisement **eye-catching**?

   colours _____

   title   _____

   illustration _____

   d What **information** will the poster give?

   _____

   _____

   _____

   price
   opening times
   where to buy
   location

   _____   _____

   _____   _____

   _____   _____

2 Write some **persuasive words and phrases** you could use on your poster.

   _____   _____   _____

   _____   _____   _____

   _____   _____   _____

UNIT 14 The Old Forest

Vocabulary

Root words, prefixes and suffixes

> Remember, a **root word** is a basic word to which **prefixes** and **suffixes** can be added to make other words from the same word family.
>
> **Root word:** comfort
>
> comfort   **un**comfort**able**   **dis**comfort
>
> comfort**able**   comfort**ing**   comfort**ed**
>
> comfort**ably**

A Complete the gaps in this table.

Root word	+ Prefix	+ Suffix
tidy		tidiest
agree		
	irregular	
happy		
		understanding

Punctuation

Direct speech round-up

> **Direct speech** is when we write the **actual words** someone has spoken. The **spoken words** go inside the **speech marks**.
>
> Pippin asked, "Where is the path?"
>
> "I can see the path!" cried Merry. "We will soon be out of the forest."

A Add any missing **speech marks** and other **punctuation** to each sentence.

1 Merry asked Can you hear that dripping noise

2 I can hear it said Pippin and feel it as well

3 Travelling through the forest is dangerous said Frodo We have to stick together

Spelling

ey word endings

Words that end in **ey** can be tricky to spell.

Usually, when we add **s** to most words ending in **y** we change the **y** to an **i** and add **es**.

However, if the word ends in a **single vowel + y** we simply add **s**.
  chimn**ey** + s = chimn**eys**

A Find **six** words ending with **ey** in the word search and write them on the lines below.

d	j	r	u	k	w	x
h	o	c	k	e	y	v
o	l	w	z	y	p	a
n	p	h	x	a	m	l
e	g	f	d	d	o	l
y	m	v	y	p	n	e
p	m	o	n	k	e	y
l	s	i	u	d	y	o

_____   _____   _____

_____   _____   _____

B Write **three** more words ending with **ey**. Use each word in a sentence.

1 _____ _____

2 _____ _____

3 _____ _____

C Circle the word with the different **letter pattern**. Write each word you have circled in its **plural form**.

1 alley   valley   journey   trolley   _____

2 jockey   donkey   turkey   chutney   _____

3 monkey   honey   chimney   money   _____

Grammar

Auxiliary verbs

Sometimes **verbs** are made up of more than one word.
The verbs **to be** and **to have** are often used with other verbs to make different **tenses**.
We call these verbs **auxiliary verbs**.

Verb **to be**:

The ground **is** rising steadily.

The ground **was** rising steadily.

They **are** entering the Old Forest.

They **were** entering the Old Forest.

Verb **to have**:

They **have** entered the Old Forest.

It **has** not taken you long to lose us.

It **had** not taken you long to lose us.

The word **auxiliary** means helper.

A Choose the correct **auxiliary verb** from the box to complete each sentence.

> am   are   is

1 The forest _____ growing darker.
2 I _____ wondering.
3 They _____ worried.
4 Merry _____ speaking.

B Underline the **verb** in each sentence. Change the verb from the present tense to the **past tense**.

                                                             past tense

1 We are reading about the old forest. _____

2 They are taking the wrong path. _____

3 That tree is leaning dangerously. _____

C Add an **auxiliary verb** to each of these verbs. Use the new verbs in sentences of your own.

1 _____ dripping   _____

2 _____ plodding   _____

3 _____ felt   _____

Writing

Characters

Frodo, Pippin and Merry have been trying to find their way out of a dark forest.

1 You are going to write the next part of the story. What do you think the characters do, say and feel when they find their way out of the forest?

   a Merry

   In the forest Merry seemed fairly cheerful and whistled with relief when he saw the path.

   Do you think Merry was more or less worried than the others? _____

   When they find their way out, what do you think Merry:

   - does? _____
   - thinks? _____
   - feels? _____

   b Pippin

   In the forest Pippin 'could not bear it any longer' and 'let out a shout'.

   Do you think Pippin was more or less worried than the others? _____

   When they find their way out, what do you think Pippin:

   - does? _____
   - thinks? _____
   - feels? _____

   c Frodo

   In the forest Frodo began to wonder if it were possible to find a way through.

   Do you think he was more or less worried than the others? _____

   When they find their way out, what do you think Frodo:

   - does? _____
   - thinks? _____
   - feels? _____

   d Use your notes to write the next part of the story in your exercise book.

UNIT 15 Rainforests in Danger

Vocabulary

Using a dictionary

The words in a dictionary are in alphabetical order but, to make it easier to find a word, there are **guide words** at the top of each page.

These tell you the first word and the last word that appear on that page.

For example, if the guide words on a page are **jovial** and **keep**, the first word on the page is 'jovial' and the last word on the page is 'keep'. The word 'jug' would be on this page.

A Here are the **guide words** from three different pages in a dictionary:

Page 128:   lost   lunch
Page 129:   lung   mail
Page 177:   racket   rare

Write the number of the page on which each of the following words would appear:

1 machine _____   2 luxury _____   3 railway _____
4 rapid _____   5 loud _____   6 loyal _____
7 ramp _____   8 luggage _____   9 range _____

Punctuation

Punctuating sentences

All **sentences** begin with a **capital letter**.

A **statement** ends with a **full stop**.
   Rainforests are important.

A **question** ends with a **question mark**.
   How can we protect the rainforests?

An **exclamation** ends with an **exclamation mark**.
   The rainforests are at risk!

A Write your own **statement** about rainforests.
_____

B Write your own **question** about rainforests.
_____

C Write your own **exclamation** about rainforests.
_____

Spelling

ar and are words

> It is important to notice the distinctive sounds **ar** and **are** words make.

A Add a word from the word box to complete each sentence. Each word can only be used once.

scarf	cards	share
spare	scared	stars

1 The car had a puncture so we used the _____ wheel.
2 Cleo offered to _____ her sweets.
3 Jah gave out his business _____.
4 The _____ were twinkling in the sky.
5 The children were _____ of the thunder.
6 The _____ matched Tamika's new top.

B Add **ar** or **are** to complete each of these words.

1 sp_____
2 st_____ting
3 ch_____t
4 y_____d
5 c_____ful
6 bew_____
7 p_____k
8 l_____ge
9 d_____k
10 sh_____p
11 sm_____tly
12 _____m
13 gl_____
14 sc_____f
15 prep_____ed

C Write three sentences. Choose two **ar** or **are** words to go in each one.

1 _____

2 _____

3 _____

Grammar

Relative clauses

To make sentences more interesting, we can use **relative clauses**.
A **relative clause**:
- begins with a **relative pronoun: who, which** or **that**
- tells us more about the **noun** or **pronoun** in the **main clause**.

For example:

These people, who cleared areas of the forest, built houses and grew crops.

Main clause: These people built houses and grew crops.

Relative clause: who cleared areas of the forest

These people moved from cities which had become overcrowded.

Main clause: These people moved from cities

Relative clause: which had become overcrowded

Who is used for people.
Which and **that** are used for animals and things.

A Underline the **relative clause** in each sentence.
1. We should protect rainforests which help the planet.
2. We should stop doing things that harm the planet.
3. We should persuade people who clear areas of rainforest to stop.

B Complete each sentence by adding a **relative clause**.
1. Do you have a book _____?
2. There are some scientists _____.
3. Is this the magazine _____?

C Write about your friend. Write two sentences and use at least two **relative clauses**.

_____
_____
_____
_____

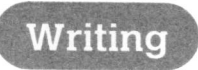

Writing for an audience

1. You are going to plan and make a **leaflet** to **persuade** young people that the rainforests must be protected.

   a. What is the title of your leaflet?
   Think of a few ideas. Choose the best one.

   _____   _____

   _____   _____

   b. Find three ways in which rainforests are being destroyed and who is destroying them. Make notes.

   • _____

   • _____

   • _____

   Make a list of the pictures you will need.

   • _____

   • _____

   • _____

   c. Find three reasons why rainforests should be protected. Make notes.

   • _____

   • _____

   • _____

   Make a list of the pictures you will need.

   • _____

   • _____

   • _____

2. Use your notes to create your leaflet.

UNIT 16 Undersea World

Vocabulary

Onomatopoeia

> **Onomatopoeia** is the word we use to describe words that sound similar to what they are describing.

A Underline the **onomatopoeic** word in each of these sentences.
1 The birds twittered in the tree.
2 There was a loud bump as the book dropped to the floor.
3 The drip of the leaky tap began to irritate Mum.
4 The lion's roar could be heard close by.
5 There was a huge splash as Tuhil jumped in the pool.

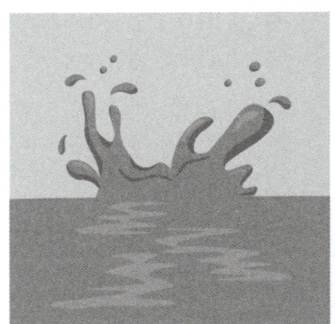

B Write **two** of your own sentences, each with an **onomatopoeic** word.
1 _____
2 _____

Punctuation

Commas after adverb clauses

> To make sentences more interesting, we can use **adverb clauses**.
> An **adverb clause** works just like an **adverb**. It tells us more about the **verb**.
> If an **adverb clause** comes **at the beginning of a sentence**, we put a **comma** after the **adverb clause** before the rest of the sentence.
> **Because corals build their homes on old skeletons**, huge reefs are formed.

A Complete these sentences with **adverb clauses**.
1 _____ we went snorkelling.
2 _____ I was very careful.
3 _____ you must not touch them.
4 _____ they tore the boats.
5 _____ we went with a guide.

Spelling

ost and oll words

Many words with a single **o** have a short vowel sound, as in **got**.

Words with the letter pattern **oll** and many words with the letter pattern **ost** have a long vowel sound.

Perhaps one the **most** amazing sea landscapes is the coral reef.

You would never know they are there as the waves **roll** over them.

A Complete each sentence with a different word from the box.

stroll   post   almost   roll

1 My grandmother enjoys a _____ in the park.

2 I _____ won, but was overtaken just before the finish line.

3 My little brother wanted to _____ the ball down the hill.

4 Will you _____ this letter for me?

B Write each of these words in a sentence.

1 scroll _____

2 post _____

3 almost _____

C Each word below has a missing **oll**, **oal** or **ole** letter pattern. Use the clues to help you complete each word. Check your answers in a dictionary.

The letter patterns **oll**, **oal** and **ole** often make the same sound.

1 a gentle walk   str_____

2 often has a flag at the top   p_____

3 a large group of fish   sh_____

4 a young horse   f_____

5 players try to score this in football   g_____

6 space left after something is taken out   h_____

Grammar

Homonyms

> **Homonyms** can be words that are **different parts of speech** but:
> - they **sound** the same
> - they are **spelled** the same
>
> For example:
>
> These **plants** are called algae.   plants = noun
>
> He **plants** rice every year.   plants = verb

A Write which **part of speech** each bold word is.

1. a I heard a **talk** about the coral reefs at school.   _____
   b My teacher told us to **talk** quietly.   _____
2. a I worked **hard** on my project.   _____
   b One type of coral is very **hard**.   _____
3. a I had a **rest** after snorkelling.   _____
   b Will you **rest** for a while?   _____

B Which **homonym** can complete both sentences in each question?

1. a I played in the _____.
   b He did not _____ the car very well.
2. a She put the _____ on her finger.
   b I heard the school bell _____.
3. a I got a part in the _____.
   b We _____ football after school.

C Write sentences to show the **two meanings** for each word.

1. head
   a _____
   b _____

2. post
   a _____
   b _____

3. race
   a _____
   b _____

Making notes

1. You are going to write a short **report** about what coral reefs are like. Read the information below and underline information you will use in your report.

2. You are going to write an **explanation** of how coral reefs are formed. Read the information below and use a different colour to underline the information you will use in your explanation.

Coral Reefs

The oceans of the world are full of the most incredible creatures. Plants, rocks and corals form weird and wonderful landscapes. Perhaps some of the most amazing landscapes are coral reefs.

The Great Barrier Reef

The Great Barrier Reef is a chain of 3,000 individual coral reefs off the coast of Queensland in northeastern Australia. It stretches for 2,300 kilometres.

The word 'reef' comes from an old word *rif*, meaning an undersea danger to ships. Sailors, sailing over the coral reef to get to shore, were very aware that the sharp corals could tear the bottom of their boats. In time, the word *rif* changed to 'reef'.

Corals and plants called algae, are some of the world's most incredible living things. These miniscule creatures build reefs which can survive even the huge waves caused by tropical storms and tsunamis.

Corals combine their strength with beauty in their colourful branching shapes.

What are corals?

Corals are composed of tiny animals called polyps. They belong to the same family as jellyfish. The polyps live in a limestone skeleton. Each polyp has a ring of tentacles around its mouth to catch food.

There are two basic types of coral – hard corals, and soft corals. Hard corals produce a limestone skeleton which forms the reef. Soft corals look much the same but they do not have a solid limestone skeleton.

How are reefs formed?

Coral reefs form when coral and algae find the right living conditions to thrive – warm, clear water and light.

They are made from limestone, formed from skeletons of millions of tiny sea animals and plants. Each new generation fastens itself to the remains of the previous generations' skeletons. The skeleton of the coral is both an anchor when the polyp is waving about in the water, and a hiding place into which it can retreat when threatened. Because corals live in huge colonies, young corals build their homes on old skeletons and, in this way, huge reefs of limestone are formed.

UNIT 17 Shipwrecked!

Vocabulary

Idioms

> **Idioms** are short phrases that usually mean something different from what you might expect.
>
> Remember, **abstract nouns** are the names of qualities, feelings or times that you can't see or touch (for example: **bravery**, **happiness**).

A For each of the **idioms** below, find the abstract noun in the box that is closest to its meaning. Use a dictionary to check the meanings of any of the words in the box that are unfamiliar to you.

> insincerity   cowardice   boastfulness   certainty
> excellence   selfishness   indecision   alertness

1 in the bag _____
2 blowing one's own trumpet _____
3 second to none _____
4 feathering one's own nest _____

B Use two idioms from **Activity A** in sentences of your own.

1 _____
2 _____

Punctuation

Punctuation round-up

> These are the **punctuation marks** that have been covered so far.
> full stop **.**   question mark **?**   exclamation mark **!**
> comma **,**   apostrophe **'**   speech marks **" "**
> dashes **—**   brackets **( )**

A **Punctuate** these sentences.

1 What are you reading Salma asked
2 Its a story *Robinson Crusoe* by Daniel Defoe replied Farah
3 Whats it like Salma asked
4 Its amazing said Farah Its about a man who was shipwrecked

Spelling

ild and **ind** words

> Words that have the spelling pattern **ild** and **ind** often have a long vowel sound.
>
> Nothing can describe the confused state of my **mind** when I sunk into the water ... At last, I was free from danger and out of the reach of the **wild** waves.

A Add **ild** or **ind** in the gaps to make a word.

Then write three sentences using three words you have written.

1 unw _____   2 m _____   3 unk _____
4 beh _____   5 w _____   6 f _____
7 rem _____   8 ch _____   9 w _____

1 _____
2 _____
3 _____

B Circle the word in each group that has a different **i** sound

1	kind	grind	print	blind	mind
2	remind	unkind	kind	behind	hint
3	child	twin	wild	mild	wilder

Remember, **prefixes** and **suffixes** are added to root words.

C Write the root word found in each of these words.

1 rewind   _____   2 minder   _____
3 grinding   _____   4 reminded _____
5 childish   _____   6 finding   _____
7 unkindly   _____   8 mildness _____

Grammar

Improving writing

> We can **improve** our writing by:
> - **changing the order of words** in sentences to avoid repetition.
>   I went down to the sea early that morning. **I** looked at the water.
>   **Early that morning,** I went down to the sea. I looked at the water.
> - using **conjunctions**
>   I looked at the water. I noticed a boat coming towards the shore.
>   I looked at the ships **and** noticed a boat coming towards the shore.

A Improve each pair of sentences by **changing the word order** so both sentences do not begin with **I**.

1 I finished my book late last night. I really enjoyed it.

_____

_____

2 I will get another book when I go to the library. I would like another adventure story.

_____

_____

B Join each pair of sentences with a **conjunction**.

1 I am doing my reading homework. I am going to the cinema.

_____

_____

2 I would like to be Robinson Crusoe. I would like to live on a desert island.

_____

_____

C Copy and **improve** these sentences.

I have to write an adventure story this weekend. I have been trying to think about what to write. I haven't come up with any ideas!

_____

_____

_____

_____

Writing in the first person

Imagine you have been washed up on a desert island.
Write about what the island is like and what you do.

1. What can you **see** on the desert island? Use interesting **adjectives** to describe:

    - the beach _____
    - the cliffs _____
    - the trees _____
    - anything else? _____
    _____

2. What can you **hear** on the desert island? Use interesting **adjectives** to describe the sound of:

    - the waves _____
    _____
    - the birds _____
    _____
    - anything else? _____
    _____

3. How do you feel on the desert island? Are you tired, frightened, relieved, interested? Any other ideas?

    _____
    _____
    _____
    _____
    _____

4. What do you do on the desert island? Do you explore, build a shelter, look for food? Any other ideas?

    _____
    _____
    _____
    _____
    _____

BOOK 5 Glossary

abbreviation when a word is shortened – for example: *telephone* becomes *phone*

antonyms words that have opposite meanings – for example: *fast* and *slow*

auxiliary verb a verb that is sometimes called a 'helper' verb because it is used with another verb to make different tenses – the verbs *to be* and *to have* are auxiliary verbs

brackets punctuation marks ((…)) that are used to add extra information in a sentence

dash a punctuation mark (–) often used to add extra information in a sentence

homonym words that sound the same and are spelt the same but have different meanings – for example: *bat* (*something used in sport and a flying animal*)

homophone words that sound the same, but are spelt differently and have a different meaning – for example: *son* and *sun*

hyphen a punctuation mark (-) that is used to join two words to make compound words (for example: *fast-moving*) or to join a prefix to a word (for example: *co-own*)

idiom a figure of speech which means something different from its literal meaning – for example: *to be over the moon* (to be delighted)

indirect speech when we write about what someone has said, without using the exact words and without speech marks

metaphor a figure of speech which describes something as if it is something else – for example: *a blanket of clouds*

modal verbs an auxiliary (helper) verb used to say what is possible, what is necessary or what is going to happen in the future – the verbs *can*, *must* and *will* are all examples of modal verbs

onomatopoeia when a word sounds like what the word describes – for example: *pop*, *splash*, *crackle*

personification when a writer gives human/animal qualities to non-livings things – for example: *the trees danced in the wind*

possessive adjective an adjective used to show ownership: *its, your, my, their, our, her, his* – for example: *my* house

pronoun a word that stands in place of a noun, used to avoid repeating the noun – for example: *he, them, it*

relative clause a clause that is added to a main clause to give more information, beginning with a relative pronoun – for example: *I caught the bus that arrived early*. In this sentence, *that arrived early* is a relative clause

relative pronoun a pronoun that takes the place of a noun and acts like a conjunction – for example: *who, which, that*

sequencing adverbs adverbs that tell us the order in which things are done – for example: *then, later, in the afternoon*

simile a figure of speech which describes something as or like something else – for example: *as bright as the sun*